Frances the Royal Family Fairy was originally published
as a Rainbow Magic special. This version has
been specially adapted for developing readers
in conjunction with a Reading Consultant.

To Lara and Isla, two wonderful sisters

Special thanks to
Rachel Elliot

ORCHARD BOOKS

This story published in Great Britain in 2015 by Orchard Books
This Early Reader edition published in 2018 by The Watts Publishing Group

1 3 5 7 9 10 8 6 4 2

© 2018 Rainbow Magic Limited.
© 2018 HIT Entertainment Limited.
Illustrations © Orchard Books 2018

A CIP catalogue record for this book is available from the British Library.

ISBN 978 1 40834 577 1

Printed in China

MIX
Paper from
responsible sources
FSC® C104740
www.fsc.org

The paper and board used in this book are made from wood from responsible sources.

Orchard Books
An imprint of Hachette Children's Group
Part of The Watts Publishing Group Limited
Carmelite House, 50 Victoria Embankment, London EC4Y 0DZ

An Hachette UK Company

Frances
the Royal Family Fairy

Daisy Meadows

ORCHARD

www.rainbowmagic.co.uk

The Fairyland Palace

Throne Room

Wetherbury Village

Contents

Story One

The Royal
Fairy Baby

Chapter One

A New Fairy Friend

Kirsty Tate and her best friend
Rachel Walker were putting
on their favourite dresses. They
had been sent a very special
invitation!

*Princess Grace and Prince Arthur are
delighted to announce the birth of their second
child. A beautiful sibling for
Prince George!*

*You are invited to celebrate the new arrival
and attend a welcoming ceremony at the
Royal Fairyland Palace.*

*Someone special will collect
you both at midday
on Saturday!*

"We are so lucky," said Rachel with a smile, pinning a sparkling clip into her hair. "This will be the second royal baby fairy ceremony we've attended in Fairyland!"

Kirsty and Rachel had been to Prince George's special ceremony. But naughty Jack Frost and his gang of mischievous goblins had tried to spoil the day.

"I hope Jack Frost behaves himself this time," said Kirsty.

"Me too," said Rachel. She looked at the clock. "It's almost midday. Who do you think is coming to collect us?

Kirsty thought about all of the fairies they had met. "It could be anyone. We're so lucky to have lots of fairy friends!"

"Hello, girls!" said a voice.

Kirsty and Rachel whirled around to see who it was.

They saw a
beautiful
fairy
standing
on the
windowsill.
She was
wearing a
silky blue dress,
and a sparkling tiara sat on her
long, dark hair.

"I'm Frances the Royal
Family Fairy," she said.

"Hello!" said Rachel with a
big smile. "Are you going to be

part of the special ceremony?"

"Yes," Frances replied, flying over to the girls. "I have a magical rubber duck wearing a crown, which helps me to watch over royal siblings. I make sure that they play happily together, share their toys and have lots of fun."

"I'm sure Prince George will be a wonderful big brother," smiled Kirsty.

Frances sprinkled fairy dust over the girls. They felt themselves shrink to fairy size.

Frances pointed her wand at
the mirror on the dressing table.
The glass began to shimmer.

"We're going to Fairyland!"
she said, with a tinkling laugh.

Chapter Two

Fairyland Friends

Hand in hand, Rachel and Kirsty fluttered through the glass. For a moment their skin felt warm and tickly. Then they opened their eyes and found themselves on the lawn of the Fairyland Palace!

The girls heard a chorus of friendly voices calling their names. A group of fairies was on the lawn, chattering and playing with Prince George and a beautiful rosy-cheeked fairy baby.

"Hello, Prince George!" said Rachel. Prince George waved a chubby hand and put his arm around the baby.

"Wow, you're a really good big brother," said Kirsty with a smile, hugging both babies and their fairy friends.

Soon it was time for the royal ceremony. In the Throne Room, the king and queen stood next to Prince Arthur and Princess Grace. Frances took her place beside them, a rubber duck in her hand.

Rachel smiled when she noticed that the duck was wearing a golden crown.

Prince George held the baby's hand and flew towards the beautiful crib. The queen welcomed everyone and then each group of fairies stepped forward in turn to give a magical gift.

The Fun Day Fairies gave the baby the gift of laughter, and the Sporty Fairies bestowed the gift of sporting skills. One by one, the fairies gave wonderful presents to the new arrival.

But then there was a loud crash of thunder and horrible Jack Frost appeared in the room!

Frances cried out as the icy ruler grabbed the rubber duck out of her hands and then vanished with a flash of blue lightning. The Royal Family Fairy's magic had been stolen!

Into the Woods

Prince George and the baby started to cry. Everyone looked shocked and upset.

Queen Titania looked at Rachel and Kirsty. "Girls, we'll need your help," she said. "This is a very serious situation.

Without Frances's rubber duck, royal siblings in the human and fairy worlds will feel very sad and won't get along with each other."

"What can we do?" asked Kirsty.

"Will you go with Frances to the Ice Castle and find the rubber duck?" the queen asked.

"Of course we will," said Rachel.

Frances and the girls flew out of the Throne Room and zoomed up into the bright sky. They knew they had to stop Jack Frost from spoiling everything.

The fairies soon arrived at Jack Frost's gloomy Ice Castle.

There was a row of rubber
ducks lined up all the way
around the top of the castle!

"Let's take a closer look
and see if your rubber duck is
there," Kirsty suggested. But
as the friends swooped down,
several goblin guards jumped
up from behind the walls. They
picked up the rubber ducks and
started throwing them at the
fairies!

"Push off, silly fairies!"
shouted one plump goblin.

As the girls zoomed around

trying to avoid the flying
rubber ducks, they spotted Jack
Frost heading out of the castle
and into the forest.

The fairies flew after him.
The forest was dark and a bit
spooky.

"We'll never find him in here!"
said Frances with a groan.

Suddenly they heard a shriek
and Jack Frost sprang up from
behind a holly bush! "What are
you doing in MY forest?" he
yelled.

"Give Frances back her
rubber duck," said Kirsty. "It's
wrong to take things that
belong to other people."

"It's mine now," snapped Jack Frost. "And it's time that everyone started talking about ME and MY sibling."

"But you don't have a brother or a sister," said Rachel, puzzled.

"I'm going to make myself a new sibling using this magic rubber duck!" cackled Jack Frost, running off into the forest. "And there's nothing you can do to stop me …"

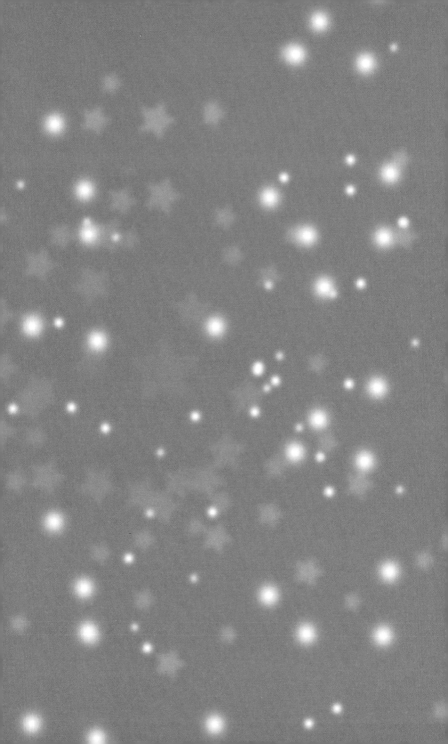

Story Two

A Sneaky Sister

Chapter One

Icy Magic ...

"This is even worse than I thought," said Frances. "He's going to use my magical rubber duck to make a brother or sister. And that sibling is bound to be horrible, just like Jack Frost!"

"Let's find him and stop

him!" cried Kirsty.

The fairies flew through the dark forest, but they couldn't spot Jack Frost. But the mean creature had used his magic to make hundreds of rubber ducks! The ducks were lined up on tree branches and peeked out from among the flowers.

"This is hopeless," said Frances with a groan.

Just then, Rachel spotted a flash of blue light through a gap between two fir trees. It was Jack Frost! He was holding Frances's magical rubber duck up in the air and saying a spell:

"Rubber ducky, make me lucky!
Create a sibling mean and yucky.
Someone who will share my dreams,
And help me with my tricks and schemes!"

There was a
rumble of thunder
and a bright-
blue flash. Then
a second figure
appeared next to
Jack Frost. She had the
same sharp nose and spiky hair.
When she saw the fairies, she
gave a mean grin.

"I'm Jilly Chilly," she said.
She raised her wand and ropes
appeared. They snaked around
the fairies, pinning their wings
and arms down by their sides!

"Ha ha!" Jack Frost said, hooting with laughter. "That's the  funniest thing I've seen all day!"

Jilly Chilly linked arms with him and they walked off together. Rachel, Kirsty and Frances were trapped!

Frances shivered. "It'll be dark soon. We have to think of

a way to get free!"

Kirsty looked around her. She thought she saw a pair of eyes peeking out from under a bush. "I think there's someone over there," she said.

Rachel nodded. "I think it's one of the animals of the forest. They might be able to help us."

"Good thinking," said Kirsty. "All animals love fairies!"

"Animals of the forest!" called Frances in a loud voice. "We really need your help. We have to get free and stop Jack Frost's nasty plans, or fairy and human royal families will suffer."

"Please help us!" added Rachel.

Chapter Two

Forest Friends

For a moment, all the friends
could hear was the breeze
rustling the leaves in the trees
around them. Then squirrels,
mice, moles and rabbits crept
out into the clearing and came
shyly towards the fairies.

They started to nibble at the ropes. After a few minutes, the ropes fell off.

"Hurrah!" Rachel exclaimed. She rubbed her arms where the rope had been. Kirsty and Frances were soon free, too.

"Thank you, friends!" cried Kirsty.

Frances picked up her wand. "We need warm clothes," she said. She waved her wand and instantly the three of them were snuggling into thick, cosy hooded capes.

"Now we have to follow Jack Frost and get the rubber duck back," said Kirsty.

The three friends waved goodbye to the helpful forest animals and flew up through the snow-covered trees.

It was getting dark, and in the

distance they could see the lights of the Ice Castle.

They zoomed towards the castle, and a few minutes later they were hovering outside the window of the Throne Room. To their surprise, they could see goblins hard at work inside. Some were hanging flowery wallpaper, while others laid a thick blue carpet on the floor. More were dusting and tidying!

"How strange," said Rachel. "I've never seen the goblins working so hard before."

"The goblins look scared," Kirsty added.

"Something strange is going on," said Rachel with a frown. "Frances, could you turn us into goblins? Then we can find out what's happening!"

Chapter Three

Cleaning the Castle

The three fairies slipped into
the castle through an open
window and hid behind a
flowery curtain. Frances waved
her wand, and the girls turned
into goblins. They had big
noses and green skin!

"Are you sure this is a good idea?" asked Frances, looking nervous. "What if they realise that you're not really goblins?"

"Don't worry," said Rachel, smiling at the little fairy. "We've had lots of practice at pretending to be goblins!"

She and Kirsty each took a deep breath and then stepped out from behind the curtain.

"You're late!" snapped a grumpy voice. "Hurry up and put on some aprons!" A thin, spotty goblin was glaring at

Rachel and Kirsty.

"Why should we?" said
Rachel, trying to sound like a
normal, rude goblin.

"Because Jilly Chilly said so,"
said the spindly goblin. "And
you don't want to get on the
wrong side of her. She's mean!"

"We saw her earlier," said Kirsty. "Jack Frost seemed to like her."

"He thinks she's wonderful," said the goblin in a gloomy voice. "He's letting her do whatever she wants – even cleaning and redecorating the castle."

"She's awful," said a short, plump goblin. "All she does is shout at us and take cold bubble baths with that silly rubber duck."

Rachel and Kirsty exchanged

excited glances. Jilly Chilly had
Frances's rubber duck!

Story Three

Rubber Ducky Rescue

Chapter One

A Chilly Bath

Rachel winked at Kirsty. "It seems as if we'd be better off without Jack Frost's new sister," she said.

"Yes, she doesn't like us at all," said a goblin with a drippy nose. "But Jack Frost thinks she's brilliant!"

"I know how we can stop him liking her so much," said Kirsty, thinking fast. "Without the rubber duck, the magic he used to create her will be very weak and he won't want a sister any more."

"We should steal the duck!" cried the short goblin at once.

"Hide it!" exclaimed the thin goblin.

"No, we should eat it!" shouted the goblin with the drippy nose.

"I think hiding it is the best idea," said Rachel in a firm voice, before the goblins started fighting. "We'll do it — she hasn't seen us before."

None of the goblins argued. Nobody wanted to go anywhere near Jilly Chilly, as she was so mean! Just then, a terrible shriek echoed through the castle.

"I want more bubbles for my bath NOW," screeched Jilly Chilly's voice.

Kirsty glanced over at the

curtains, where she knew
Frances was hiding. She put her
hands behind her back.

"Luckily, I've got some
amazing new bubble
bath," she said
in a loud voice,
hoping that
Frances would
hear her and
use her magic

to make some bubbles! Her
plan worked and a large bottle
of bubble bath appeared in
Kirsty's hands.

"We'll take this to Jilly Chilly now," said Rachel. "Then we'll try to get the rubber duck."

Rachel and Kirsty waved goodbye to the other goblins and hurried along the corridors, following the sound of splashing water and Jilly Chilly's screeching voice.

"I hope that Frances waits for us in the Throne Room,"

said Kirsty as they ran.

"She will," said Rachel.
"She'll have heard our plan."

They arrived at the
bathroom and pushed open
the door. The floor was covered
with water, and wet towels lay
all around. In the centre of the
room was a large bath, and
Jilly Chilly was sitting in it.

Her fists were clenched and she was thumping the edge of the bath and kicking her legs crossly!

Chapter Two

A Perfect Plan

"You two horrible goblins had better have some more bubbles for me!" shouted Jilly Chilly.

The girls poured the bubbles into the bath. They saw that bobbing around Jilly Chilly was a little rubber duck wearing a golden crown!

"I'm going to make waves," said Jilly Chilly. "Watch this!"

She started to slide backwards and forwards in the bath. The waves grew higher and higher! Water splashed across the floor and bubbles landed on everything – including Rachel and Kirsty. But they were watching the little rubber duck. It flew up into the air and Kirsty reached out her hand and caught it.

"Let's go!" she called excitedly to Rachel.

Still looking like goblins, the girls ran along the corridor.

They were halfway to the Throne Room when they heard Jilly Chilly shriek.

"Where's my rubber ducky?" she screamed. "BRING IT BACK!"

At last the girls saw the Throne Room up ahead. They burst through the door, where the other goblins were waiting for them.

"We got it!" Kirsty yelled. The goblins cheered and Kirsty

saw Frances dart out of the
window into the
night. Kirsty
hurled the
rubber duck
through the
window
after the little
fairy, and then
stopped, gasping
for breath. Rachel was close
behind her.

Suddenly the Throne Room
door flew open again, and Jack
Frost sprang into the room.

He was frowning. "Who's making that terrible racket?" he demanded.

"JILLY CHILLY!" shouted all the goblins together – even Rachel and Kirsty.

"Well, I can't live with someone who makes that sort of noise!" Jack Frost thundered.

"I'm going to reverse that spell right now and send her away. Little sisters are really ANNOYING!"

The goblins started cheering. They were so pleased that mean Jilly Chilly was going away!

Rachel and Kirsty slipped over to the window and peered out.

Frances was hovering outside, holding her rubber duck in her hand.

"Well done, both of you!" she exclaimed happily. "Let's get out of here."

Chapter Three

Happy Families

With a wave of her wand,
Rachel and Kirsty became
fairies once again. The girls and
Frances shared a big hug.

"I think it's time we went
back to the Fairyland Palace,"
said Frances.

As they zoomed away from the Ice Castle, the sky became clearer and the stars and moon appeared. Soon they saw the beautiful Fairyland Palace ahead of them. They flew down and made their way to the Throne Room.

The king and queen were talking quietly, and the royal babies were playing happily together. When the guests saw Frances, Rachel and Kirsty arrive, they started to clap. Princess Grace came hurrying

towards the girls, holding out
her hands.

"Thank you from the bottom
of my heart," she said. "I knew
you must have succeeded as
soon as the babies became
friends again."

"Our family is happy again,"
added Prince Arthur, "and
royal families all over the
human world are safe too —
thanks to you."

Rachel and Kirsty curtseyed,
and then they shared another
hug with Frances.

Soon it was time for them to
go home. Frances waved her
wand, and everything started to
shimmer and shine.

A few moments later Rachel
and Kirsty were standing
in front of Kirsty's dressing
table, and the sun was shining

through the window. They were human-sized again and were wearing their pretty dresses.

"I'm so pleased that royal families are all happy again," said Rachel. "Isn't it great that we were able to help?"

Kirsty nodded. Just then, her bedroom door opened and her mum looked in. "Oh, what lovely dresses!" she exclaimed. "Are you playing a dressing-up game? I just wanted to tell you that there are fairy cakes and lemonade downstairs for you."

She left, and the girls smiled
at each other. Time stood
still when the girls were in
Fairyland and so Mrs Tate
didn't know about their travels
to Fairyland!

"I'm so happy that we
have such magical adventures

together," said Rachel, hugging her best friend.

"Me too," said Kirsty. "And I'm so happy that I'm able to share them with you!"

The End

**If you enjoyed this story,
you may want to read**

Catherine the Fashion
Princess Fairy
Early Reader

Here's how the story begins ...

One sunny Saturday, best
friends Rachel Walker and
Kirsty Tate were standing in
a crowd outside a beautiful
palace. The girls were visiting
the city for the weekend with
Kirsty's parents and they were

waiting to meet a family friend, Bee, when she had finished work. Bee was a fashion stylist and was inside the palace at that very moment!

Kirsty smiled up at the palace. "It must be fantastic to help the princesses decide what to wear every day," she said.

"Definitely!" agreed Rachel, linking arms with Kirsty.

Everyone loved the three princesses who lived in the palace, but the youngest – Princess Edie – was the girls' favourite!

"It's very different from the Fairyland Palace, isn't it?" Kirsty whispered.

Rachel smiled, thinking of the beautiful pink palace where Queen Titania and King Oberon lived. The girls had been special friends of Fairyland for a long time!

"I hope that we get to see the Fairyland Palace again soon," said Rachel.

"You may see it sooner than you think," said a silvery voice.

The girls jumped in surprise.

A pretty little fairy had appeared on the gate of the palace! She was wearing a flowing green dress with a matching hat. Glossy brown hair coiled over her shoulder.

"Hello!" she said. "I'm Catherine the Fashion Princess Fairy!"

"Hi, Catherine," said Kirsty. "What are you doing here?"

"I've come to find you," said Catherine. "There's a problem in Fairyland – please will you help?"

"Of course we will," said

Rachel at once. "But there are people everywhere! How can we be magicked to Fairyland?"

Kirsty looked around and smiled. "I've got an idea," she said, pointing to a large postbox nearby. "Let's slip behind there. We'll be hidden from sight!"

Read
Catherine the Fashion Princess
Early Reader
to find out
what happens next!

Meet the first Rainbow Magic fairies

Can you find one with your name?
There's a fairy book for everyone at
www.rainbowmagicbooks.co.uk

Let the magic begin!

Become a
Rainbow Magic
fairy friend and be the first to
see sneak peeks of new books.

There are lots of special offers and exclusive
competitions to win sparkly
Rainbow Magic prizes.

Sign up today at
www.rainbowmagicbooks.co.uk